I0133977

The Thoughts of a Prophet

Copyright © 2013 by Prophet Clinton C. Chambers

All Rights Reserved. No part of this book may be used or reproduced in any manner whatsoever without prior written permission except in the case of brief quotations embodied in critical articles or reviews.

ISBN: 978-0-9891732-6-1

Rocket Press Publishing, LLC
139B James Comeaux RD. # 571
Lafayette, LA 70508

Visit our website at:
www.RocketPressBooks.com

Email us:
info@rocketpressbooks.com

First Edition
10 9 8 7 6 5 4 3 2

Printed in the United States

THE THOUGHTS OF A

PRPHET

———— SOUND WISDOM AND PRECIOUS INSIGHT ————

THE THOUGHTS OF A
PR⬤PHET

———— SOUND WISDOM AND PRECIOUS INSIGHT ————

ROCKETPRESS
PUBLISHING

Prophet Clinton C. Chambers

DEDICATION

This Book is dedicated to my Family both Natural and Spiritual. To the Chambers & Millners Family, to my God fearing and Loving Mother Ms. Mae L England, my Brothers and Strength Deacon Dennis W. Millner, Bro. Charles Chambers, my Baby Sister and Prayer Warrior Sis. Gaye D. England, my Son Clinton Chambers 3rd, my Daughters Ny'Asia, Aseanti, Ceaira, Shekinah, Tiffany and to all of my Grandchildren Nieces and Nephews! To Prophetess Tiwana Alexander (Prayer Warrior, Support & Friend), Rev. & Mother Rufus Johnson (God Parents) Bishop W.S. Rouse, Pastor Stella Mercado & Blanche Memorial Church Jamaica,NY, Mother Doris Hill (Godmother), Pastor & Lady Robinson & Gateway COGIC South Ozone,NY, Pastor & Lady Pearson & 2nd Bethlehem Church St. Albans,NY, Bishop Brehan Hall & Greater New Psalmist Church Toledo,Ohio, Bishop & Lady McGhee & Serenity Church Toledo,Ohio, Bishop & Lady Gay & Higher Way Ministries Petersburg,Va., Pastor Darla Freeman Alexander & Testimony of Jesus Ministry Atlanta,Ga, Pastor & Lady Sturdivant & New Meltonville MB Church, Monroe,NC, Pastors Kenneth & Maryann Lane & Ultimate Power Revival Center#2, Summersville,SC, Apostle Lloyd Benson & Cathedral World Worship Center Baton Rouge,La, Pastor & Lady Little & Praise Temple Arcadia,La , I Thank God for All of you! I Love you ALL!

TABLE OF CONTENTS

Chapter 1

I

Men With Integrity

Integrity. What is it really? Webster defines "integrity" as "firm adherence to a code of moral values", "incorruptibility", "completeness", "and soundness", "an unimpaired condition". These are just some of the definitions found for integrity. Integrity is very important to God. It is this attribute that singles out or sets apart men and women of the clergy. We need integrity in all areas of our lives. It is somewhat of a commodity nowadays because life itself has to be faced head on with integrity and truth. Someone once said that "Honesty is the best policy". That still holds true today.

So why is integrity important in the pulpit? Why is it important in the home? Let us ponder on this for a few minutes.

In speaking with a number of pastors and husbands, I have learned that there are special characteristics involved in making a good pastor and a good husband. Most of my conversations were with those who held both titles; pastor and husband. When I asked about what makes a good pastor, I recall that a good pastor is one who must be a good follower of God before he himself can be followed. A good pastor has to maintain his integrity at all times. When you are at the helm and a focal point for so many people, the way you walk is very imperative and must be consistent. A good father also must walk in integrity every day. He is viewed as his son or daughter's hero; his wife's knight in shining armor; and so many other things to many people. A good pastor must be consistent in the Word of God. Their opinion cannot sway, but must be lined up with that of the Bible. Their opinion must mirror what is outlined in God's word. It is a covenant relationship and must be adhered to as sacred and like no other relationship.

Men with integrity must possess attentiveness to themselves and others. They must watch how they walk and how they speak. Living with integrity means: Not settling for less than what you know you deserve in your relationships. Asking for what you want and need from others. Speaking your truth, even though it might create conflict or tension. Behaving in ways that are in harmony with your personal values. Making choices based on what you believe, and not what others believe. Even fathers must walk in integrity, but must not lose sight of their place in the home. Often times, pastors tend to forget how to be husbands. They are consumed with their pastoral call; so much to the point where they do not embrace fatherhood. What must be realized is that just because you are a pastor and a father, it means that our children are heirs of ours; not heirs to the church. What we must remember is Jer. 29:11 says "For I know that plans I have for you, saith the Lord". Whatever God has for you, it is for you. God's plan always triumphs over any other plan. What a pastor and a husband must be is sensitive in both capacities; without letting it take away from their masculinity.

Often times, a pastor and a husband without integrity will lack in fatherhood, companionship, finances, compassion and a number of other important qualities. Without integrity, a pastor cannot be a proper husband. As pastors/preachers, we must learn to honor our mates. The bible reminds us in Proverbs 18:22: "Whoso findeth a wife findeth a good thing, and obtaineth favour of the Lord". It is not just important to be a "good" pastor or husband, but there are many responsibilities that go along with that. I Timothy 5:8 says: "But if any provide not for his own, and especially for those of his own house, he hath denied the faith, and is worse than an infidel". Simply put, if a pastor/husband does not provide and do what is right by his congregation or family, he is not worthy of the title "pastor" and "father". There is more to being a pastor and a father. It has nothing to do with putting on the proper attire, or with consummation. God makes men of integrity!

We have been taught for many years that "real men don't cry!" Perhaps that is a matter of opinion, but the reality of it is that real men always have a backup plan. When things do not go according to orchestration, then a new plan of operation must be put in place. As pastors and men of integrity, we have to put love in its proper place. The church is the Bride. When one takes a bride, they treat that bride with utmost respect. They honor her and nurture her with love like they loved no other. What a lot of pastors and men in general fail to realize is that our loving God is contingent upon how we treat our companion. We all know the scriptures about how a husband must treat his wife like Christ does the church and all that. What we must realize is that when a man possesses integrity, he learns how to be a man of the cloth, a father, a confidante, and a friend.

Men of integrity wear many hats. These hats cannot be worn by just anybody. A man of integrity is ordained by God to be that. When a man walks with integrity, it becomes his calling card for life. He is identified by the attributes that mirror God. In other words, self is denied and God's will and truth prevail. A man of integrity is not selfish and does not mind being under tutelage that will thrust him further into ministry, or life in general. A man of integrity does not feel that he knows it all; but rather, is willing to learn more so that he can be the man of God that he was ordained and "hand-picked" to be.

Here are a few quotes regarding integrity that I thought were profound:

"Integrity is doing the right thing, even if nobody is watching."

— Jim Stovall

"Integrity is telling myself the truth. And honesty is telling the truth to other people."

"Never do anything that you can't admit doing, because if you are that ashamed of whatever it is, it's probably wrong."

"Living a life of integrity is one of the greatest missions we can undertake."

"Speak your truth with grace and integrity, even though it might upset some people. You never know who else, besides yourself, it might help."

NOTES

_____
_____
_____
_____
_____
_____
_____
_____
_____
_____
_____
_____
_____
_____
_____
_____
_____
_____
_____
_____
_____
_____
_____
_____
_____
_____
_____
_____
_____
_____

NOTES

_____

_____

_____

_____

_____

_____

_____

_____

_____

_____

_____

_____

_____

_____

_____

_____

_____

_____

_____

_____

_____

_____

_____

_____

_____

_____

_____

_____

NOTES

_____

_____

_____

_____

_____

_____

_____

_____

_____

_____

_____

_____

_____

_____

_____

_____

_____

_____

_____

_____

_____

_____

_____

_____

_____

_____

_____

_____

_____

_____

Chapter 2

II

Spirit of Poverty

Webster defines "poverty" as "want of earthly goods". Other words that describe it are: destitution, deficit, debt, depletion, starvation, reduction, emptiness. These are just a few of the words that come to mind when we think of poverty. What I have come to understand is that poverty is not just a state of being, but it is also a condition and a spirit. When the spirit of poverty is prevalent, it causes a person to feel inept, incomplete and lost. From a spiritual point of view, spiritual poverty can be viewed as worse than poverty in the natural. Let me explain.

I read an article on this subject, and here are a few excerpts from it:

Spirit of poverty is like a clawing monkey on the back of many Christians who love the Lord, but who cannot seem to get a handle on their finances. They attend financial classes at church and nod their heads in agreement. But, when the rubber meets the road, they are unable to apply the biblical truths to their own pocketbooks. Sometimes, self-deception prevents these well-meaning souls from obeying godly principles. I have spoken with people who think their tithed is complete for the past year, only to receive their annual statement from the church and find they have fallen way short with their giving.

Why? Honestly, I don't know which comes first. Does the lack of application of biblical principles lead to a spirit of poverty or does a spirit of poverty make it hard to apply biblical principles, even though the heart is willing?

When a Christian is living in a spirit of poverty, there is a continual drain of money. It constantly disappears, flowing out the proverbial window. When money comes in, no matter how much, it slowly trickles or quickly pours away. There is nothing left to show for it. If this is a pattern in your life, then you may be operating in a spirit of poverty. Another clue is that no matter what the income, there never seems to be enough to pay the bills and take care of life's expenses. There is always a need for more money, more income, and a higher credit limit. *[End of article]*

Now this article is based on the financial part of poverty. What I want to discuss is the tree of poverty. Poverty is like a tree with many branches. On this tree, you may have the following branches:

☐ Defeat

☐ Loss

☐ Weakness

☐ Insecurity

☐ Anger

☐ Hurt

☐ Separation

And the list goes on! These branches continue to grow and the tree of poverty gets bigger and bigger. As more and more emphasis is made on the branches themselves; in other words, the more we as Christians give in and over to these branches, the stronger the tree gets. After a while, the spirit of poverty takes total control and all is lost. The scripture tells us:

All hard work brings a profit, but mere talk leads only to poverty," (Proverbs 14:23 NIV)

This is merely letting us know that talk is cheap! It also implies that if we're only going to talk about a thing, there will be no progress; and if there be no progress, hence, there will be POVERTY!

Now, one might ask themselves: "How does this happen?" "How does it start?" And more importantly, "How do we get rid of it?"

To start, we must remember that in order for there to be a deficit with anything, there has to first be the realization of what was in the beginning. For it to get to this state of poverty (spiritually), we had to have lost our way at some point.

The minute we decide to serve God and Him only, we open the door to the enemy's vices and distractions. One sure way to distract a believer is to mess with their faith. When things are going well with believers, all is right with the world. But the minute we get opposition or things start to unravel, we began to have doubt, fear, anxiety, stress and all those negativities that gnaw at our Christian stature.

If we are accustomed to believe that prayer changes things that are the weapon we will use when the enemy strikes. If we are accustomed to believe that there is no problem too big for God to solve, that is when the enemy begins to attack our minds. If we allow the enemy to weaken our walk with God by simply whispering "sweet nothings" in our ear all the time, when God gets ready to speak to us, we cannot hear properly because we have allowed the enemy to dictate to us.

The tree of poverty's branches will grow with each weakening moment the believer allows the enemy to have free course in their life. When we stop believing that God can heal, deliver, set free, restore, revive, etc., that is the perfect opportunity for another branch to sprout out on this tree of poverty!

Speak those things that be not as though they were — Romans 4:17

We have to learn to speak life into our circumstances! Sometimes we cannot help but fall victim to the branches on this tree of poverty because it is something that has been handed down from one generation to another. Those are called "generational curses". This is the enemy's way of making us adapt to hindrances and roadblocks that will cause us to miss out on the things that God really has in store for us. Jeremiah 29:11: For I know the plans I have for you, saith God. He knows what He wants for us before we even know it, and before He even reveals it! The enemy also knows God's plans. If he doesn't know them "specifically", he at least knows that God has a plan. When we take our eyes off of God, we allow the enemy to come in and entertain us. This puts us at a very big disadvantage because now we have lost our focus.

Basically, the only way to rid ourselves from the poison from these branches is to completely allow God to minister to our hearts, souls, minds and bodies. We have to be still and hear the audible voice of God. We must learn to tune out all those things, people, issues, etc., that will alienate us from hearing God's voice. We all have a sense of purpose and our lives are designed for greatness. That is always the will of God; to see us go forth and prosper. What happens to that plan is that we fall victim to the enemy's vices and lose sight of what is important and vital to our spiritual growth. Once our spiritual growth is threatened (dried out), we die at the root and fall off. *(See St. John 15:1-6)*

I am the true avine, and my Father is the husbandman.

2 Every abranch in me that beareth not bfruit he taketh away: and every branch that beareth fruit, he cpurgeth it, that it may bring forth more fruit.

3 Now ye are clean through the word which I have spoken unto you.

4 aAbide in me, and I in you. As the branch cannot bear fruit of itself, except it abide in the vine; no more can ye, except ye abide in me.

5 I am the avine, ye are the branches: He that abideth in me, and I in him, the same bringeth forth much fruit: for without bme ye can do nothing.

6 If a man aabide not in me, he is cast forth as a branch, and is withered; and men gather them, and cast them into the fire, and they are burned.

Once they are burned; there is no more life left in them. That is why we must tap into the giver of life who will replenish, restore, rejuvenate and revive us! As long as we let the branches on this tree of poverty dictate, our lives will be fruitless and bare and we will not be able to abide in Him.

We must abide in the vine that will bring us good things; good fruit; branches on that vine will be prosperity, peace, love, joy, increase, power, anointing and so many gifts we won't have room to receive them!

The Bible also tells us in St. Matthew 5:3 it reads:

"Blessed are the poor in spirit for theirs is the kingdom of heaven".

What it is to be poor in spirit?

To have a realizing sense of our spiritual state. In this it is implied that we understand our own guilt and helplessness, and realize as a practical fact our own utter emptiness by nature of every thing good, and of any tendency to that which is good. It is one thing to hold this in theory, and another thing to be heartily sensible of the humbling fact. Most professing Christians admit in words that they are in themselves wholly helpless and destitute, but to know and feel as an abiding practical conviction that this is their true spiritual condition how few are able!

Being poor in spirit implies that we see in its true light the tendency in us to every thing evil--that we understand that the habitudes of our minds, that our appetites and tendencies, that nearly the whole power of the sensibility continually tends to selfishness.

Now ask: Why are the poor in spirit "blessed"?

Because in a sense, such a person has already learned what the remedy is: He has learned to reject himself, and that his dependence must be utterly and forever on another than himself. He has learned how blessed it is to be nothing, to know and do nothing of himself, to be universally dependent upon Christ for every thing--for breath, for grace, for faith, for every thing; to have Christ his "all and in all."

Because they learn how blessed it is to trust Christ: They see such fullness in Christ, they do not wish any strength of their own. Their wisdom, righteousness, sanctification and redemption are in Christ, and they need and wish for none of their own. Christ is all they need, and they need nothing in themselves. They have them all in Christ, and they are willing and glad to have them in him.

Because they have learned how to be composed in the midst of all kinds of trials: They neither have nor seek any resort in themselves. They know in whom their strength lies, and who their strong tower is. They can depend on Christ for all, and they know He cannot and will not fail them.

Because they have no self interest: They have seen themselves to be perfectly destitute and worthless. They have no reputation to build up, they have no appetite that must be gratified, no passion that must be catered for, none of these to contend for or hold on to. They are emptied out, and every particle of self value is gone entirely. They labor not for themselves, but for Christ.

Because to be poor in spirit is to be rich in faith: Then poor in the proper sense emptied of dependence upon themselves, then they are rich in faith!

So you see, once we realize that the branches on this tree of poverty can easily be broken off by totally leaning and depending on God, we can chop the tree down completely. The branches will cease to exist in our lives because we have replaced them with faith and total commitment to God!

So, there you have it. You know how this tree is sown; and you know how to kill it. The choice is ours today. I say: choose "life" and abide in the Vine (which is Jesus Christ)!

NOTES

NOTES

_____
_____
_____
_____
_____
_____
_____
_____
_____
_____
_____
_____
_____
_____
_____
_____
_____
_____
_____
_____
_____
_____
_____
_____
_____
_____
_____
_____

Chapter 3

III

The Relevance of Order, Obedience and Overflow!

Ezekiel 34th Chapter

In today's Christian society, we have many people who are being led astray and are falling victim to spirits of destruction. If people are not careful who they are led by, or who they allow to be their leader, many will fall by the wayside and into peril. Let's discuss, for a few moments, the qualities of a good leader.

God wants complete order in our lives. The way we eat, talk, love, work, worship, etc. We are to obey the will of God and follow his commands, keep His commandments, which will result in an overflow in our lives.

Order comes with a good leader. A good leader has an exemplary character. It is of utmost importance that a leader is trustworthy to lead others. A leader needs to be trusted and be known to live their life with honestly and integrity. A good leader "walks the talk"; and not so much "walks the walk" (we have enough people mimicking God's people as it is!) But in doing so, a good leader earns the right to have responsibility for others. True authority is born from respect for the good character and trustworthiness of the person who leads.

A leader also needs to function in an orderly and purposeful manner in situations of uncertainty. People look to the leader during times of uncertainty and unfamiliarity, and find reassurance and security when the leader portrays confidence and a positive demeanor.

Good leaders are tolerant of ambiguity and remain calm, composed and steadfast to the main purpose. Storms, emotions, and crises come and go and a good leader takes these as part of the journey and keeps a cool, calm demeanor.

Obedience to God is vital for a Christian to prosper. God knows what He wants for us. (Jeremiah 29:11) Our lives have already been orchestrated by God. We must learn to trust Him completely and allow Him free reign in our lives so that we can be the sons and daughters He is looking for.

Not everyone who claims to be a Christian is a Christian. Only those who are in a genuine relationship with Christ are the true Christians. Those who know Christ will want to obey him and follow His will. This does not mean that a believer will always do the right things or never sin. It only means that believers have been changed by God's grace and now WALK in relationship with Him, following Him and living the life that He lived to the best of their ability.

One of the main reasons God wants us to be obedient is that He knows what is best for us, but He also wants us to live the good life of obedience, holiness and purity. I Thessalonians 4:3 says, "It is God's will that you should be sanctified; that you should avoid sexual immorality. " Sanctified means "set apart" for God. We are in a special relationship with God and because God is holy, He wants us also live holy lives that are pleasing to Him. I Thessalonians 4:8 says, "For God did not call us to be impure, but to live a holy life." He has called us to this type of obedience because He loves us, and wants what is best for us.

When we make up our mind to be obedient to God and to His divine order of things, we will begin to see blessings in our lives unfold. Our vision becomes clearer; we now know where God is taking us, and what He is allowing us to become in Him! We no longer rely on the promises of man; who merely holds up (hinders) what God has designed for us.

It is in this New Year that God has shown me that many leaders are going to be restored in a time such as this. The enemy has declared war on those carrying God's word; those with a charge, but God is still on the throne! Jesus is still sitting at the right hand of the Father; making intercession for you and for me. There is no reason for the leaders of God's people to feel forgotten and rejected by God. That is the trick of the enemy to distract our leaders, and cause them to lose their focus.

That is why it is imperative that we understand God's leading. When we put things in their proper order and perspective, we are more willing to be obedient. Why? Because we now see WHERE WE ARE GOING! I have learned that when people have a visual picture of where they are being led, they will conform more easily than they would if they were not given a glimpse of their impending victory!

In Ezekiel the 34th chapter, what we see happening is simply this: From the first to the sixth verse, we see the rulers restored. The people were like sheep gone astray; without a shepherd. That is how many of God's people feel today. We feel like we are sheep that have been given up as prey for the enemy. When this happens, our spiritual life becomes like a desolate land. When God's people go through an experience like this, their trust and faith in God's word is tried and tested and because they lack the faith they should have, their heart is sometimes hardened, or simply not motivated to do the Lord's work.

From the seventh to the sixteenth verse, we now see the people restored to their own land. God intended mercy for this scattered flock. This is also referring to the restoration of His chosen people, the Jews. This is how a good shepherd (leader) shows tender care for the souls of his people. A good shepherd will look for his people wherever they are, whether it is darkness (natural), or spiritual darkness (ignorance), he will find them and bring them into the fold. This is how our Lord and Savior Jesus Christ is towards us. He is the Good Shepherd who loves us and leads us into righteousness. Because of how He treats us, it causes us to rest on His love. We will, however, have those who think it is solely because of what THEY have done for the people, that brings restoration and reproof to them. For those presumptuous folk, He will cut them down to size. For his disquieted saints, He will bring us rest.

Finally, from the seventeenth to the thirty-first verse, we realize the restoration of the Kingdom of Christ. The whole nation appears to be the Lord's flock, but yet there are those who are different, or carry themselves in a whole different way. Notice the words in these verses "good pastures" and "deep waters"; that simply means the Word of God being "pure", and shelling out "justice". The rest of those verses speak about the prophesy of Christ and all that we as believers can expect being His! It speaks about glorious times to be had right here on earth! As long as we are under our Good Shepherd, this body of believers (the Church) would be a blessing to all. Christ; the tender plant, being the Tree of Life, bearing all fruits of salvation, He himself yields spiritual food to the souls of His people. He feeds us!

So what results can we expect from being subservient to Order, and from yielding in Obedience that such order? The answer to that is OVERFLOW!!

God's people are rewarded with the divine Overflow of blessings! This overflow can be represented by people, prosperity, growth, revelation, restoration, increase, extension, elevation and all of the promises that God has ordained for the people of God! The bible teaches us in Hebrews 11:6: But without faith it is impossible to please him: for he that cometh to God must believe that he is, and that he is a rewarder of them that diligently seek him. God wants to bless His people. As with a child and obedience, once that child yields to the order of his parent, and is obedient to what he has been asked or directed to do, the only response should be a reward.

Romans 15:13 speaks about overflow. Now may God, the source of hope, fill you with all joy and peace as you believe, so that you may overflow with hope by the power of the Holy Spirit. This is what the overflow is all about. In this New Year of 2012, the people of God should awaken with a spirit of expectation! We should now be mindful of who we are in God, and what it is we possess.

Because of what we possess, we should walk more freely into our inheritance and promise.

When Jesus was here on this earth, He said that He came to give us "abundant life" (John 10:10). This is a life that is overflowing with all the blessings of the Spirit of God. He tells us that when we trust Him, we will be like that artesian well. Our life will literally gush with the overflow of His work within us. (John 4:14.

We have earned the overflow! Now, because of the power that God has imparted in us, we can simply demand the overflow to happen in our lives! We now have carte blanche on what we want for our lives from God. The cattle on a thousand hills belong to Him! Walking into our overflow means that in ADDITION TO WHAT IS RIGHTFULLY OURS, THERE'S MORE!!! Are you ready for THE MORE?? CAN YOU STAND TO BE BLESSED EVEN MORE??

So, now you should be able to comprehend the importance and relevance of order, obedience and overflow. This is the year of Order, Obedience and Overflow!

NOTES

NOTES

Chapter 4

IV

The Spirit of Whoredom

"For the spirit of whoredoms have caused them to err, and they have gone a whoring from under their God."
-Hosea 4:12.

Many times, when we hear the word "whoredom", the first thing that comes to mind is a sin of a sexual nature. Words like "lust", "fornication", "promiscuity" and the like come to mind. But let us first define "whoredom" from the natural point of view, and then we will address the spiritual point of view, as well.

"Whoredom" is defined in Webster's New Collegiate Dictionary" as *sexual immorality; idolatrous practices; the practice of whoring; and prostitution"*.

What we must understand is that the works of the spirit of whoredoms are manifest, and they are harlotry, idolatry, love of the world, love of money, love of food, love of the body, love of position, and unrighteousness. I guess it is fair to say that our entire human race can be found guilty of the spirit of whoredom because nobody is perfect, and we are not in a glorified body; hence, we may possess many, if not all of these traits. What is also important is that the spirit of error goes hand in hand with the spirit of whoredom. When one is governed by the spirit of error, it gives way to all of these other spirits and they operate in unison with one another. For instance, error will cause the instance of prostitution, unfaithfulness, unchaste, backslidden state, strong affection or devotion to an object or a person, temptation, lust, fornication, adultery, sexual immorality of any type, etc... Once these spirits have been entertained, sexual immorality becomes an idol in your life; fornication and adultery will be your God, and it will instruct you in the way you should go. It will totally consume you because it is a spirit.

When the spirit of whoredom takes over, it will cause you to deviate from the divine plan of God in your life. You no longer allow God's spirit and guidance to maneuver you; but rather, you indulge in faithless, unworthy and idolatrous practices or pursuits. Now, instead of being the faithful, Christian, baptized believer that God called you to be, you are now operating in a hypocritical mindset. It is almost as if you have been replaced with robotic gestures that yield "temporary" satisfaction. You find yourself oftentimes trying to compromise with what you are doing; trying to justify the immoral acts you perform, or involve yourself in; all the while making deals with yourself for deliverance at some point.

Whoredom means simply that your will has been taken over; compromised and altered so that you no longer go by what God has mandated, but rather you now allow yourself to be in bondage to all the above vices aforementioned. The Bible tells us that we should never let anything (or anyone) separate us from the love of God. *(Romans 8:39)* When we allow the spirit of whoredom to consume us, it opens the door to many other spirits that will ultimately destroy you. That is why we must guard ourselves daily with the Word of God. The Bible teaches in *Isaiah 26:3*: "Thou wilt keep him in perfect peace whose mind is stayed on thee". Simply put, if we keep our minds on Christ, we leave no room for the enemy to come in and take over us. "Let this mind be in you, that was also in Christ Jesus" (Philippians 2:5). When we take our eyes off the prize, and forget all the promises of God, we have just allowed the enemy to declare war on us, and we have become prey to his vices. We become vulnerable and weak. We are like "putty in his hands". We find ourselves doing things we would never have done. We may even hear things come from our lips that we never imagined uttering before.

We must learn that we possess a power above all power! We are more than conquerors through Him that have that loved us! There is another spirit that is also at work in our lives sometimes and that is the spirit of bondage. It is a terrible thing to be in bondage, or to feel as if you are bound by something. Bondage causes one to feel locked up, restricted, suffocated, limited and without freedom.

BUT!

Our Bible tells us in St. John 8:36: "He who the Son sets free, is free indeed"! We can be confident that once we are free in Christ, we are free indeed. We must mind the things of the spirit that keep us free from sin and bondage. Sin separates us from God; God's word and power connect us to Him! We must learn to set our affections on things above (heavenly), and not on things below (sinful, earthly, fleshly pleasures). When we rise above the situations that are in our lives, and allow God free reign to rule and super-rule in us, we become stronger and wiser in our choices. When our choices and decisions improve, our life improves and becomes more fruitful. We must walk in love, honor, righteousness, meekness, temperance, courage and most of all, wisdom. When we walk circumspectly, God is pleased with us.

In closing, let us remember what the scripture tells us in *2 Cor. 7:1*:

Having therefore these promises . . . let us cleanse ourselves from all filthiness of the flesh and spirit, perfecting holiness in the fear of God.

When we have been cleansed from the spirit of whoredom, let us make room only for those things that will keep us fortified, revived, rejuvenated, anointed and doing the things God has inspired and ordained us to do.

Philippians 4:8-9 (King James Version (KJV)

8Finally, brethren, whatsoever things are true, whatsoever things are honest, whatsoever things are just, whatsoever things are pure, whatsoever things are lovely, whatsoever things are of good report; if there be any virtue, and if there be any praise, think on these things.

NOTES

NOTES

_____
_____
_____
_____
_____
_____
_____
_____
_____
_____
_____
_____
_____
_____
_____
_____
_____
_____
_____
_____
_____
_____
_____
_____
_____
_____
_____
_____
_____

NOTES

Chapter 5

V

Hear

Hear, my son, and receive my sayings, And the years of your life will be many. I have taught you in the way of wisdom. I have led you in the right path. Proverbs 4:10-11

Respect the foundational ingredients in which integrity is built on, Integrity the key source needed to from one place to another. However, how does one even gain the understanding of the two without the spiritual guidance and a understand of the faith required to move within each of these is the things that hold all these ingredients together to establish the future of the church.

One thing is clear and that is the foundational characteristic of the church have been watered down and weakened to provide a diluted taste of the reality of life. The moral values have decaying with each generation and there appears to be no way of repair. One thing is clear is the church has become the last place where integrity, respect and self discipline is being demonstrated and taught. " A wise person is hungry for knowledge, while the fool feeds on trash" Proverbs 15:14

It is time to realize what the past was, how the present looks and the possibility of what the future will look like. The past is the definition of what integrity was the present is what the integrity has become and the future of what integrity has become because it has been lost in the translation of the life.

Who will teach the generation of the importance of finding and having a voice in a time where there is no power to be heard. Who will show the son of tomorrow how important their voice will be to someone else one days the one that you see every day, the bus driver, mailman, He is supposed to be the foundation of the family. The provider and the caregiver the source of knowledge and safe.

These time must be redefined be establishing the spiritual elements needed to create and establish the structure of family. The family foundation has be altered and even challenged. Not just the family of two parents and children but also the church family. The goals have been transformed and the tools that provide the build the structure has been replaced with false values and doctrine that has been altered to meet the needs of society and the true and living God.

"Jesus told them, I am the way the truth and the life. No one can come to the Father except through me." John 14:6 . Men stand up and take your place among the shoulders of the fathers before you.

NOTES

_____
_____
_____
_____
_____
_____
_____
_____
_____
_____
_____
_____
_____
_____
_____
_____
_____
_____
_____
_____
_____
_____
_____
_____
_____
_____
_____
_____
_____
_____
_____
_____

NOTES

NOTES

Chapter 6

VI

Side Notes

Side note to my Brothers:

My Brothers god has created us to Lead, this doesn't mean to Dictate, and be Controlling! There's a difference between Manipulating and Leading! Manipulating and a Deceitful spirit are the same and they're not from God!! God wants us to lead by living a lifestyle worth following! Real Men are committed to Following and obeying the will of God, not their own Will! My brothers know that because you were born male doesn't make you a Man, your chronological age doesn't make you a Man, accepting your Responsibilities makes you a Man but accepting Christ makes you a Man of God! Men of God don't duck and run from their Obligations and Responsibilities, Men of God are Fathers not Baby Daddies! Men of God don't hide from bill collectors they pay their Debts, Men of God most importantly have a Strong and Stable Relationship with God, because they know that in order to have any other Productive Relationships they must first have a Good Relationship with God! My brothers know that when God blesses you with a Woman of God and know it is a Blessing, its imperative that you cover her not Control her! You must handle her with care, she's a direct gift of God, and know that when you're bless to have Children rather you share the same DNA or not it's important that you properly Sow good seeds into their life, they are your legacy! My brothers it's time we Man up and Lead our family with Love, Prayer & Faith! Blessings

Side note to my Sisters:

My dear and precious sisters, Know that you are so very valuable sometimes more than you give yourself credit for! You are a diamond, not just a gem but the most valuable and most sought after gem a Diamond! It takes a trained eye to even locate a Diamond because when it's mined it sometimes appear to look like other stones but it's not, then it takes a Skilled Craftsman to cut away all of the outer layers and get to the Heart of the Gem then comes the Work the Cultivating of the Diamond! It doesn't matter how you may have started out, True Diamonds always start out Rough, you are still a Precious Diamond and you can't allow just anyone to handle you! Be patient and wait for that one that God has blessed with that Trained Eye, to see you for who you truly are! Also know that until he comes it's imperative that you position yourself to be received, this is done by staying focus on God! You must stop focusing on the Mistakes of your Past and begin to focus on the Promises of your Future! So many times you give into the Voices of those who really don't see you as the Precious Diamond that you are, Never allow anyone to define you other than being what you are a Diamond! God created you to shine, no matter how dim the lights are around you, your brilliance still shines! Diamonds hold its Value without a ring, a ring only displays the Diamond! That being said know that without the hair being done, without the makeup, without the pedicure and manicure you're still Valuable and Precious!! You're a Woman of God, you don't have to expose your body to be seen, a True Man of god has a skilled eye and he can see a Diamond even in the rough stages! Besides as a Woman of God your True Beauty is your Heart! Your heart and your desire to be Pleasing to God make you Beautiful!!! You've lived through your past Hurts, Heartaches, Headaches, Disappointments, Discouragements, Disasters, Putdowns, and Letdowns Now it's time for you Live the Life god has Promise and Planned for you to Live! I speak Life into your Atmosphere, You Shall Live! Live the life of a Diamond to be Honored, Admired and Loved!! Blessings

My Thoughts To Preachers:

Preachers you've been assigned to an Awesome Task, and that is to preach the Word of God!! But you can't just preach it you are Required to Live it! The Word of God before it's preached to anyone it should first stop by your house! It's easy and always effective to preach what you Know and Live! Also Preachers every Preacher has to have a Pastor, someone you've served faithfully someone who has mentored and Spoken into your life! Please know that because you've been called to Preach doesn't mean you've been called to Pastor!! It's important that you know the area of Ministry you were called to, and your Pastor will help bring clarity there! don't rush out trying to make a name for yourself, set under your Pastor and allow God to Saturate you with His Word and His Wisdom and when it's time for you to make a move you'll go with the Blessings of your Pastor and the Blessings of God, that's Order! There are some important lessons you need to learn at home like Patience, How to Serve, how to Give without looking for a return, there are so many things that you can only learn properly under the Leadership of your Pastor, so enjoy the time you're there and Learn, Learn, and then Learn some more! Now with Reality shows and Mega churches everyone wants their name up in lights, so many want to live the lifestyle of a Celebrity but you must stay Focus to the Plan of God for your Life!! Gods plan for you is just for you, and no one can do it better than you! It's good to Gleam from other Preachers but never attempt to be like anyone except Christ! Now please know that Full time Ministry isn't for everybody it's a great Sacrifice and it's not something you want to rush into because you see others do it or because it seems lucrative. I promise you if you're Faithful, Prayerful, Committed to His Plan, and stay Focus on his Will you will experience unmerited Joy!

NOTES

_____

_____

_____

_____

_____

_____

_____

_____

_____

_____

_____

_____

_____

_____

_____

_____

_____

_____

_____

_____

_____

_____

_____

_____

_____

NOTES

ABOUT
PROPHET CHAMBERS

Prophet Chambers has been in ministry for 25yrs, his ministry has been heard and seen across America and has reached, South Africa, Germany, and South America Prophet Chambers has been seen on several Christian Networks as well as his own show on the Word Network, " A Prophetic Voice" he is also heard daily on www. reign1035radio.com He is widely known for his Deliverance Ministry, where countless numbers of people have been Healed and Delivered! His ministry style has been called one that's Upfront and Direct! Prophet Chambers has received numerous awards and honors for his work with broken communities and his work with and time with broken men and women. He has a heart for those whom others have cast aside and Forgotten, he is widely known for being a Pastors Friend! It's often said that when he speaks to a person it's as if his voice penetrates directly to their Soul!

Prophet Chambers is in Covenant with Drs. Michael & Dee Dee Freeman who are also his Spiritual Parents.

ACKNOWLEDGMENTS

I am so very Thankful to God for allowing me the opportunity to share my Thoughts, and to all of those that have imparted into my life over the years, Church of Christ Disciples of Christ Northeastern Jurisdiction for laying the foundation in my youth, to Pastors A.L & Liz McCreary and the Holy Ghost Revival COGIC for introducing me personally to Salvation, to COGIC for Teaching me the Principles and Lifestyle of Holiness and for licensing my ministry, to the Baptist Pastors and Churches in Baltimore who Nurtured me during my difficult years, and to my Pastors my Covering and my Spiritual Parents Drs. Michael & Dee Dee Freeman who received me just where I was and imparted covered and loved me to a place in my life and ministry that I've never experience before!!! Blessings on all of you it's because of you that I am who I am today!

ROCKETPRESS
PUBLISHING™
www.RocketPressBooks.com

www.ingramcontent.com/pod-product-compliance
Lightning Source LLC
LaVergne TN
LVHW021546080426
835509LV00019B/2864

* 9 780989 173261 *